EMMANUEL JOSEPH

The Infinite Frontier, How Billionaires Are Reinventing Countries Through Innovation and Crypto

Copyright © 2025 by Emmanuel Joseph

All rights reserved. No part of this publication may be reproduced, stored or transmitted in any form or by any means, electronic, mechanical, photocopying, recording, scanning, or otherwise without written permission from the publisher. It is illegal to copy this book, post it to a website, or distribute it by any other means without permission.

First edition

This book was professionally typeset on Reedsy.
Find out more at reedsy.com

Contents

1. Chapter 1: The Dawn of the Crypto Revolution — 1
2. Chapter 2: The Rise of the Billionaire Innovators — 3
3. Chapter 3: Crypto and the Future of Finance — 5
4. Chapter 4: Building the Blockchain Ecosystem — 7
5. Chapter 5: Reinventing Governance Through Decentralization — 9
6. Chapter 6: The Social Impact of Crypto Innovation — 11
7. Chapter 7: The Environmental Implications of... — 13
8. Chapter 8: Redefining Wealth and Ownership in the Digital... — 15
9. Chapter 9: The Role of Billionaires in Shaping the Crypto... — 17
10. Chapter 10: Crypto and the Future of Work — 19
11. Chapter 11: The Intersection of Crypto and Artificial... — 21
12. Chapter 12: Crypto and the Global Economy — 23
13. Chapter 13: Navigating the Regulatory Landscape — 25
14. Chapter 14: The Future of Financial Inclusion — 27
15. Chapter 15: The Cultural Impact of Cryptocurrencies — 29
16. Chapter 16: Lessons Learned from the Crypto Pioneers — 31
17. Chapter 17: Envisioning the Future of Innovation and Crypto — 33

1

Chapter 1: The Dawn of the Crypto Revolution

In the early 21st century, the world witnessed the birth of a groundbreaking financial phenomenon: cryptocurrency. Originating as a decentralized digital currency, Bitcoin paved the way for an entirely new financial system. The brainchild of the mysterious figure known as Satoshi Nakamoto, Bitcoin was designed to operate independently of any central authority, relying instead on a peer-to-peer network and cryptographic proof. This revolutionary concept captured the imagination of technologists and visionaries around the world, sparking a movement that would challenge traditional financial institutions and redefine the very nature of money.

The rise of Bitcoin marked the beginning of a new era in finance, one characterized by transparency, security, and decentralization. Early adopters and enthusiasts recognized the potential of this nascent technology to disrupt the status quo and democratize access to financial services. As more people began to understand the underlying principles of blockchain technology, a growing community of developers, investors, and entrepreneurs emerged, eager to explore the possibilities of this digital frontier.

The initial years of the cryptocurrency revolution were marked by rapid innovation and experimentation. New digital currencies, or altcoins, were created to address specific use cases and improve upon the limitations of Bitcoin. Ethereum, for example, introduced the concept of smart contracts, enabling the creation of decentralized applications (dApps) that could operate autonomously on the blockchain. This breakthrough opened the door to a myriad of new possibilities, from decentralized finance (DeFi) platforms to non-fungible tokens (NFTs) that represented ownership of unique digital assets.

As the crypto ecosystem continued to evolve, the world began to take notice. Governments, financial institutions, and multinational corporations started to explore the potential of blockchain technology and digital currencies, recognizing their potential to drive efficiency, reduce costs, and create new revenue streams. The dawn of the crypto revolution set the stage for a paradigm shift in the global financial landscape, laying the foundation for a future where innovation and technology could reshape economies and empower individuals like never before.

2

Chapter 2: The Rise of the Billionaire Innovators

As cryptocurrencies gained traction, a new breed of billionaires emerged, driven by a shared vision of harnessing innovation to reshape the global economy. These visionary leaders saw the potential of digital currencies and blockchain technology to revolutionize traditional industries and create new opportunities for growth. Figures like Elon Musk, Jeff Bezos, and Vitalik Buterin became synonymous with the crypto revolution, using their wealth and influence to drive change and inspire a generation of entrepreneurs.

Elon Musk, the enigmatic founder of Tesla and SpaceX, has been a vocal advocate for the adoption of cryptocurrencies. His tweets and public statements have often sent shockwaves through the market, influencing the value of digital currencies like Bitcoin and Dogecoin. Musk's interest in crypto goes beyond mere speculation; he envisions a future where digital currencies play a central role in the global financial system. His investments in blockchain technology and commitment to promoting its adoption have cemented his position as a key player in the crypto space.

Jeff Bezos, the founder of Amazon, has also recognized the transformative potential of blockchain technology. Under his leadership, Amazon has explored various applications of blockchain, from supply chain management to cloud computing. Bezos's forward-thinking approach has positioned Amazon as a leader in the digital economy, leveraging the power of blockchain to enhance efficiency and drive innovation. His support for crypto initiatives has further solidified his reputation as a pioneer in the tech industry.

Vitalik Buterin, the co-founder of Ethereum, is another influential figure in the world of crypto. As a programmer and visionary, Buterin saw the limitations of Bitcoin and sought to create a more versatile and scalable blockchain platform. Ethereum's introduction of smart contracts revolutionized the crypto space, enabling the development of decentralized applications (dApps) that operate autonomously on the blockchain. Buterin's work has had a profound impact on the industry, inspiring countless developers and entrepreneurs to explore the possibilities of blockchain technology.

These billionaire innovators have played a crucial role in shaping the future of cryptocurrencies and blockchain technology. Their investments, entrepreneurial endeavors, and public advocacy have brought mainstream attention to the crypto space, driving innovation and fostering a culture of experimentation. By challenging the status quo and pushing the boundaries of what is possible, they have paved the way for a new era of economic growth and technological advancement.

3

Chapter 3: Crypto and the Future of Finance

The advent of cryptocurrencies heralded a new era in financial innovation, with the potential to democratize access to wealth and financial services. Digital currencies like Bitcoin and Ethereum have introduced a decentralized financial system that operates independently of traditional banks and financial institutions. This new paradigm has opened up a world of possibilities, enabling individuals and businesses to transact, invest, and save in ways that were previously unimaginable.

One of the most significant developments in the crypto space is the rise of decentralized finance (DeFi) platforms. DeFi leverages blockchain technology to create a financial ecosystem that is open, transparent, and accessible to anyone with an internet connection. By removing intermediaries and enabling peer-to-peer transactions, DeFi has the potential to reduce costs, increase efficiency, and provide financial services to underserved populations around the world. Platforms like Uniswap, Aave, and Compound have gained popularity for their innovative approaches to lending, borrowing, and trading digital assets.

Stablecoins are another important development in the world of crypto finance. These digital currencies are pegged to stable assets like the US dollar, providing a reliable store of value in an otherwise volatile market. Stablecoins offer the benefits of cryptocurrencies, such as fast and low-cost transactions, without the price fluctuations that can deter mainstream adoption. Projects like Tether, USD Coin, and Dai have gained traction as trusted stablecoins, facilitating cross-border transactions and providing a stable medium of exchange.

The future of finance is also being shaped by the integration of cryptocurrencies into traditional banking and payment systems. Financial institutions like PayPal, Visa, and Mastercard have begun to embrace digital currencies, enabling their customers to buy, sell, and transact with crypto. This growing acceptance of digital currencies by mainstream financial institutions is a testament to their potential to revolutionize the global financial landscape.

As the crypto ecosystem continues to evolve, it is clear that digital currencies and blockchain technology will play a central role in the future of finance. By democratizing access to financial services, reducing costs, and fostering innovation, cryptocurrencies have the potential to create a more inclusive and efficient global financial system. The journey has just begun, and the possibilities are limitless.

4

Chapter 4: Building the Blockchain Ecosystem

Blockchain technology, the backbone of cryptocurrencies, has proven to be a game-changer in numerous industries beyond finance. As the technology matured, it became evident that its potential applications were vast and far-reaching. This chapter delves into the development of the blockchain ecosystem, from its early days to the present. Early adopters recognized that blockchain's decentralized and immutable nature could be harnessed to address challenges in various sectors, leading to a surge of innovation and experimentation.

One of the first industries to embrace blockchain was supply chain management. Companies like IBM and Walmart implemented blockchain solutions to enhance transparency, traceability, and efficiency in their supply chains. By recording every transaction on a decentralized ledger, businesses could ensure the authenticity and integrity of their products, from production to delivery. This innovation not only improved operational efficiency but also built trust with consumers who demanded greater accountability.

Healthcare is another sector that has benefited from blockchain technology. The secure and transparent nature of blockchain makes it an ideal solution for managing sensitive patient data and medical records. Projects like MedRec and Estonia's e-Health system have demonstrated the potential of blockchain to streamline healthcare processes, reduce fraud, and improve patient outcomes. By providing a tamper-proof record of medical history, blockchain empowers patients with greater control over their health data and facilitates seamless information sharing among healthcare providers.

Digital identity verification is yet another promising application of blockchain. Traditional identity verification methods are often cumbersome, prone to fraud, and reliant on centralized authorities. Blockchain offers a decentralized and secure alternative, enabling individuals to manage and share their identity information with confidence. Initiatives like Sovrin and uPort are paving the way for a future where digital identities are portable, secure, and universally recognized.

The role of billionaires and tech giants in driving blockchain adoption cannot be overstated. Visionaries like Bill Gates, Jack Ma, and Richard Branson have invested heavily in blockchain projects, recognizing their potential to transform industries and create new economic opportunities. Their support has accelerated the development of the blockchain ecosystem, fostering a culture of innovation and collaboration that continues to push the boundaries of what is possible.

5

Chapter 5: Reinventing Governance Through Decentralization

One of the most profound impacts of blockchain technology and cryptocurrencies is their potential to revolutionize governance. Traditional governance models often suffer from inefficiencies, lack of transparency, and centralization of power. Blockchain offers an alternative approach, leveraging decentralized autonomous organizations (DAOs) and smart contracts to create more inclusive and transparent decision-making processes.

Decentralized autonomous organizations operate on a blockchain, allowing stakeholders to participate in governance without the need for intermediaries. Decisions are made through a consensus mechanism, ensuring that all voices are heard and that the interests of the community are prioritized. DAOs have been successfully implemented in various contexts, from managing investment funds to coordinating large-scale projects. The Ethereum-based DAO, for example, demonstrated the potential of this innovative governance model, despite facing challenges and setbacks.

Smart contracts are another powerful tool for decentralized governance. These self-executing contracts automatically enforce the terms and conditions agreed upon by the parties involved. By eliminating the need for intermediaries, smart contracts reduce the risk of fraud, increase efficiency, and enhance transparency. They have been widely adopted in various sectors, including finance, real estate, and supply chain management, to automate processes and ensure compliance with predetermined rules.

Real-world examples of decentralized governance can be found in the efforts of blockchain-based voting systems. Traditional voting methods are often criticized for their susceptibility to fraud, lack of transparency, and inefficiency. Blockchain offers a secure and transparent alternative, enabling tamper-proof voting and real-time result verification. Projects like Follow My Vote and Voatz have demonstrated the potential of blockchain to enhance the integrity of electoral processes and increase voter trust.

While the promise of decentralized governance is undeniable, it also comes with its own set of challenges. Ensuring security, scalability, and user adoption are critical factors that must be addressed to realize the full potential of this innovation. Moreover, ethical considerations such as privacy, accountability, and inclusivity must be carefully navigated to create governance models that truly benefit all stakeholders.

6

Chapter 6: The Social Impact of Crypto Innovation

Beyond the financial and technological realms, cryptocurrencies and blockchain technology have the potential to drive significant social change. These innovations are being leveraged to address pressing global issues such as poverty, inequality, and access to education. By providing new tools and opportunities, crypto innovation is empowering individuals and communities around the world to improve their lives and create a more equitable future.

One of the most promising applications of blockchain technology is in the realm of financial inclusion. Traditional banking systems often exclude marginalized populations, leaving them without access to essential financial services. Cryptocurrencies offer an alternative, enabling individuals to transact, save, and invest without the need for a bank account. Mobile-based crypto wallets and peer-to-peer lending platforms are providing financial services to millions of unbanked and underbanked individuals, particularly in developing countries.

Blockchain technology is also being used to enhance transparency and accountability in charitable organizations. By recording donations and expenditures on a decentralized ledger, blockchain ensures that funds are used as intended and that donors can track the impact of their contributions.

Projects like BitGive and Alice are pioneering the use of blockchain for charitable purposes, creating a more transparent and efficient philanthropic ecosystem.

Access to education is another area where blockchain and crypto innovation are making a difference. Educational platforms like ODEM and BitDegree leverage blockchain to provide affordable, accessible, and verifiable learning opportunities. By issuing blockchain-based certificates and credentials, these platforms enable learners to showcase their skills and knowledge to potential employers with confidence. Additionally, blockchain-based scholarship programs and decentralized education funding models are helping to break down financial barriers and create new opportunities for students worldwide.

Philanthropic organizations and social enterprises are at the forefront of driving social change through crypto innovation. Billionaires like Bill Gates, Richard Branson, and Jack Dorsey have committed significant resources to supporting blockchain-based projects that address global challenges. Their efforts are not only creating positive social impact but also inspiring a new generation of entrepreneurs and innovators to leverage technology for the greater good.

7

Chapter 7: The Environmental Implications of Cryptocurrencies

While cryptocurrencies offer numerous benefits, their environmental impact has become a topic of increasing concern. The energy consumption associated with cryptocurrency mining, particularly Bitcoin, has raised questions about the sustainability of digital currencies. This chapter delves into the environmental challenges and opportunities within the crypto space, exploring the efforts of innovators and companies dedicated to reducing the carbon footprint of digital currencies.

Cryptocurrency mining involves solving complex mathematical problems to validate transactions and secure the network. This process, known as proof-of-work, requires significant computational power and energy consumption. As the popularity of cryptocurrencies has grown, so too has the demand for energy, leading to concerns about the environmental impact of mining operations. Bitcoin mining, in particular, has been criticized for its high energy consumption, which rivals that of entire countries.

In response to these concerns, the crypto community has been exploring alternative consensus mechanisms that are more energy-efficient. Proof-of-stake, for example, is a consensus algorithm that selects validators based on the number of tokens they hold and are willing to "stake" as collateral. This approach significantly reduces the energy required to secure the network, making it a more sustainable alternative to proof-of-work. Ethereum's transition to a proof-of-stake consensus mechanism, known as Ethereum 2.0, is a notable example of this shift towards sustainability.

Innovators are also developing new technologies and practices to mitigate the environmental impact of cryptocurrency mining. Renewable energy sources, such as solar and wind, are being used to power mining operations, reducing their reliance on fossil fuels. Additionally, initiatives like carbon offset programs and eco-friendly mining hardware are helping to minimize the carbon footprint of the crypto industry.

While the environmental challenges of cryptocurrencies are significant, they also present an opportunity for innovation and positive change. By adopting more sustainable practices and technologies, the crypto community can address these concerns and pave the way for a greener future. Moreover, the transparency and traceability of blockchain technology can be leveraged to promote environmental accountability and drive sustainable development in various industries.

8

Chapter 8: Redefining Wealth and Ownership in the Digital Age

The rise of cryptocurrencies has fundamentally altered our understanding of wealth and ownership. Digital assets, such as non-fungible tokens (NFTs), are revolutionizing the way we perceive and interact with valuable items. This chapter explores how NFTs and other digital assets are reshaping the concept of ownership and creating new opportunities for creators and investors alike.

Non-fungible tokens are unique digital assets that represent ownership of a specific item or piece of content. Unlike traditional cryptocurrencies, which are interchangeable, NFTs are indivisible and cannot be replicated. This uniqueness has made NFTs particularly popular in the art and entertainment industries, where they are used to tokenize digital artwork, music, videos, and even virtual real estate. By providing a verifiable record of ownership on the blockchain, NFTs enable creators to monetize their work and connect with their audiences in new and innovative ways.

The art world has been one of the earliest adopters of NFTs, with artists and collectors embracing the technology to buy, sell, and trade digital artwork. High-profile sales, such as Beeple's "Everydays: The First 5000 Days," which sold for $69 million at a Christie's auction, have brought mainstream attention to the potential of NFTs. Digital artists now have the opportunity to reach a global audience, bypass traditional gatekeepers, and receive royalties from secondary sales, thanks to smart contracts embedded in the NFTs.

The entertainment industry is also exploring the potential of NFTs to create new revenue streams and engage fans. Musicians, filmmakers, and content creators are leveraging NFTs to tokenize their work, offering exclusive content, experiences, and collectibles to their audiences. By providing a direct connection between creators and consumers, NFTs are fostering a more decentralized and democratized creative economy.

Beyond the arts and entertainment, NFTs are being used to tokenize real-world assets, such as real estate and luxury goods. This tokenization process allows for the fractional ownership of high-value assets, making them more accessible to a broader range of investors. For example, a piece of real estate can be divided into multiple NFTs, each representing a share of ownership. This democratizes access to investment opportunities that were previously reserved for the wealthy elite, providing new avenues for wealth creation and diversification.

The gaming industry has also embraced NFTs, integrating them into virtual worlds and creating new economic ecosystems. In-game assets such as characters, items, and land can be tokenized as NFTs, allowing players to buy, sell, and trade these assets on blockchain-based marketplaces. This has given rise to the concept of "play-to-earn," where players can earn real-world income through their participation in virtual economies. Games like Axie Infinity and Decentraland have demonstrated the potential of NFTs to create vibrant and self-sustaining digital economies.

As digital assets continue to gain traction, they are challenging traditional notions of ownership and value. The concept of scarcity, once limited to physical assets, is now being applied to digital items, creating new forms of wealth and investment opportunities. This shift towards a digital-first economy is reshaping industries and redefining the way we perceive and interact with valuable items. As NFTs and other digital assets become more mainstream, they are likely to play an increasingly important role in the global economy, offering new possibilities for creators, investors, and consumers alike.

9

Chapter 9: The Role of Billionaires in Shaping the Crypto Landscape

Billionaires have played a pivotal role in the development and adoption of cryptocurrencies and blockchain technology. Their investments, entrepreneurial endeavors, and public advocacy have brought mainstream attention to the crypto space, driving innovation and fostering a culture of experimentation. This chapter highlights the contributions of key figures such as Elon Musk, Michael Saylor, and Jack Dorsey, who have used their wealth and influence to promote the widespread adoption of digital currencies.

Elon Musk, the founder of Tesla and SpaceX, has been a prominent advocate for cryptocurrencies. His public endorsements and investments in digital currencies like Bitcoin and Dogecoin have had a significant impact on the market, influencing prices and driving mainstream interest. Musk's vision for the future of finance includes a central role for digital currencies, and his companies have integrated crypto into their operations, accepting Bitcoin as payment and exploring blockchain-based solutions.

Michael Saylor, the CEO of MicroStrategy, has been another influential figure in the crypto space. Saylor's decision to invest a significant portion of his company's treasury into Bitcoin marked a turning point for institutional adoption of digital currencies. His advocacy for Bitcoin as a store of value and hedge against inflation has resonated with other corporate leaders, inspiring a wave of institutional investments in the crypto market. Saylor's commitment to promoting Bitcoin adoption has made him a key player in the ongoing evolution of the digital currency landscape.

Jack Dorsey, the co-founder of Twitter and CEO of Square, has also been a vocal proponent of cryptocurrencies. Under his leadership, Square has made significant investments in Bitcoin and developed products and services that facilitate the use of digital currencies. Dorsey's belief in the transformative potential of blockchain technology has driven his efforts to promote financial inclusion and empower individuals through decentralized solutions. His work in the crypto space reflects a broader vision of leveraging technology to create a more equitable and accessible financial system.

These billionaire innovators have not only brought mainstream attention to cryptocurrencies but have also played a crucial role in shaping the future of the industry. Their investments, public endorsements, and commitment to promoting innovation have accelerated the development of the crypto ecosystem, paving the way for a new era of financial inclusion, efficiency, and transparency.

10

Chapter 10: Crypto and the Future of Work

As cryptocurrencies and blockchain technology continue to evolve, they are also transforming the nature of work and employment. The decentralized and borderless nature of digital currencies has created new opportunities for remote work, gig economy models, and decentralized finance (DeFi) platforms. This chapter explores how these innovations are reshaping traditional employment structures and creating new opportunities for workers around the globe.

Remote work has become increasingly prevalent in recent years, driven by advancements in technology and changing attitudes towards work-life balance. Cryptocurrencies have further enabled this trend by providing a seamless and secure method of cross-border transactions. Workers can now receive payments in digital currencies, eliminating the need for costly and time-consuming international bank transfers. This has opened up new opportunities for freelancers, contractors, and gig workers to participate in the global economy, regardless of their location.

Decentralized finance platforms are also revolutionizing the way individuals access financial services and employment opportunities. DeFi platforms like MakerDAO, Compound, and Aave enable users to lend, borrow, and earn interest on digital assets without the need for traditional financial intermediaries. These platforms create new avenues for passive income and investment, empowering individuals to take control of their financial futures. Additionally, DeFi platforms are creating opportunities for developers, marketers, and other professionals to contribute to the growth and development of the crypto ecosystem.

The gig economy has also been transformed by the rise of cryptocurrencies and blockchain technology. Decentralized platforms like Bitwage and Opolis enable gig workers to receive payments in digital currencies, providing greater flexibility and financial autonomy. Blockchain-based platforms like Origin Protocol and Ethlance are creating decentralized marketplaces where workers can offer their services, connect with clients, and receive payments in cryptocurrencies. These platforms eliminate intermediaries, reduce transaction fees, and create a more transparent and efficient labor market.

As the future of work continues to evolve, cryptocurrencies and blockchain technology are playing a central role in shaping new employment opportunities and financial models. By enabling borderless transactions, decentralized finance, and gig economy platforms, digital currencies are creating a more inclusive and flexible labor market. The ongoing development of the crypto ecosystem is likely to drive further innovation and transformation in the world of work, offering new possibilities for individuals and businesses alike.

11

Chapter 11: The Intersection of Crypto and Artificial Intelligence

The convergence of cryptocurrencies, blockchain technology, and artificial intelligence (AI) has the potential to drive unprecedented innovation across various industries. This chapter delves into the ways in which AI is being integrated into the crypto space, from algorithmic trading to predictive analytics. By examining key projects and initiatives, readers will gain a deeper understanding of how the synergy between these technologies is unlocking new possibilities and reshaping the future of innovation.

Algorithmic trading is one of the most prominent applications of AI in the crypto space. AI-powered trading bots leverage machine learning algorithms to analyze market data, identify patterns, and execute trades with speed and precision. These bots can operate 24/7, making split-second decisions that maximize profits and minimize risks. Companies like Coinrule, 3Commas, and CryptoHopper have developed AI-driven trading platforms that enable users to automate their trading strategies and achieve consistent results.

Predictive analytics is another area where AI is making a significant impact. By analyzing vast amounts of data from blockchain transactions, social media, and market trends, AI algorithms can generate insights and forecasts that inform investment decisions. Platforms like Santiment and TokenAnalyst use AI to provide real-time data analysis and market predictions, helping investors navigate the complex and volatile world of cryptocurrencies. These tools empower users to make informed decisions and capitalize on emerging trends.

AI is also being integrated into decentralized finance (DeFi) platforms to enhance security, efficiency, and user experience. Machine learning algorithms can be used to detect and prevent fraudulent transactions, assess credit risk, and optimize lending and borrowing rates. Projects like Aavegotchi and Fetch.ai are pioneering the use of AI in DeFi, creating intelligent agents that interact with blockchain networks and execute tasks autonomously. These innovations are driving the next generation of DeFi platforms, offering new possibilities for financial services and applications.

The intersection of crypto and AI is also fostering innovation in other areas, such as supply chain management, healthcare, and digital identity verification. AI-powered blockchain solutions can enhance transparency, traceability, and efficiency in supply chains, reducing costs and improving operational performance. In healthcare, AI algorithms can analyze medical data stored on blockchain networks to provide personalized treatment recommendations and improve patient outcomes. Digital identity verification systems can leverage AI to enhance security and streamline identity management processes.

The synergy between cryptocurrencies, blockchain technology, and artificial intelligence is unlocking new possibilities and driving innovation across various industries. As these technologies continue to evolve and integrate, they are likely to reshape the future of innovation, creating new opportunities and challenges for individuals, businesses, and societies.

12

Chapter 12: Crypto and the Global Economy

Cryptocurrencies are increasingly influencing the global economy, with both positive and negative implications. This chapter explores the ways in which digital currencies are impacting international trade, monetary policy, and economic stability. By examining real-world examples and case studies, readers will gain a balanced perspective on the potential benefits and risks associated with the widespread adoption of cryptocurrencies on a global scale.

International trade has been significantly impacted by the rise of cryptocurrencies. Digital currencies offer a fast, secure, and cost-effective method of cross-border transactions, reducing the reliance on traditional banking systems and intermediaries. Cryptocurrencies like Bitcoin and stablecoins like USDC are being used by businesses to facilitate international payments, streamline supply chains, and enhance transparency. This has the potential to reduce transaction costs, increase efficiency, and promote economic growth, particularly in emerging markets.

Monetary policy is another area where cryptocurrencies are having a profound impact. Central banks around the world are exploring the concept of central bank digital currencies (CBDCs) as a way to modernize their monetary systems and enhance financial inclusion. CBDCs are digital versions of traditional fiat currencies, issued and regulated by central banks. Projects like China's Digital Yuan and the European Central Bank's Digital Euro are paving the way for the widespread adoption of CBDCs, offering a secure and efficient method of digital payments that can complement or replace cash.

The widespread adoption of cryptocurrencies also poses challenges for economic stability and regulation. The decentralized and borderless nature of digital currencies makes them difficult to regulate, leading to concerns about money laundering, tax evasion, and financial crime. Governments and regulatory bodies are grappling with the need to strike a balance between fostering innovation and ensuring the integrity of the financial system. The evolving regulatory landscape will play a critical role in shaping the future of cryptocurrencies and their impact on the global economy.

While the rise of cryptocurrencies presents both opportunities and risks, it is clear that they are becoming an integral part of the global economic landscape. By enabling faster, cheaper, and more secure transactions, digital currencies have the potential to drive economic growth and promote financial inclusion. As the crypto ecosystem continues to evolve, it will be essential for policymakers, businesses, and individuals to navigate the complexities and harness the benefits of this transformative technology.

13

Chapter 13: Navigating the Regulatory Landscape

As cryptocurrencies and blockchain technology continue to grow in prominence, regulatory frameworks are evolving to address the unique challenges and opportunities they present. Governments and regulatory bodies around the world are working to develop policies that protect consumers, prevent financial crime, and promote innovation. This chapter explores the current state of crypto regulation, highlighting key policies and initiatives that are shaping the future of the industry.

One of the primary challenges in regulating cryptocurrencies is their decentralized and borderless nature. Traditional regulatory approaches, which rely on centralized authorities and jurisdictional boundaries, are often ill-suited to address the complexities of the crypto space. Regulators are experimenting with new strategies to strike a balance between fostering innovation and ensuring the integrity of the financial system. Examples of these strategies include anti-money laundering (AML) and know-your-customer (KYC) requirements, which aim to prevent illicit activities and promote transparency.

Different countries have adopted various approaches to regulating cryptocurrencies. Some, like Japan and Switzerland, have embraced digital currencies and developed comprehensive regulatory frameworks that encourage innovation while protecting consumers. Others, like China and India, have taken a more cautious approach, imposing strict regulations or outright bans on certain crypto activities. The United States has adopted a mixed approach, with different regulatory bodies such as the Securities and Exchange Commission (SEC) and the Commodity Futures Trading Commission (CFTC) playing key roles in overseeing the industry.

International collaboration is also essential in developing effective regulatory frameworks for the crypto space. Organizations like the Financial Action Task Force (FATF) and the International Monetary Fund (IMF) are working to establish global standards and promote cooperation among countries. By sharing best practices and coordinating efforts, regulators can address the challenges posed by the decentralized and borderless nature of digital currencies.

As the regulatory landscape continues to evolve, it will be crucial for policymakers, businesses, and individuals to stay informed and adapt to changing requirements. By navigating the complexities of crypto regulation, stakeholders can harness the benefits of digital currencies while mitigating the risks and ensuring a secure and transparent financial system.

14

Chapter 14: The Future of Financial Inclusion

One of the most promising aspects of cryptocurrencies is their potential to promote financial inclusion for underserved populations around the world. Traditional banking systems often exclude marginalized communities, leaving them without access to essential financial services. Cryptocurrencies and blockchain technology offer an alternative, enabling individuals to transact, save, and invest without the need for a bank account. This chapter delves into the ways in which digital currencies are being leveraged to provide financial services to the unbanked and underbanked.

Mobile-based crypto wallets and peer-to-peer lending platforms are revolutionizing financial inclusion by providing affordable and accessible financial services. In regions with limited banking infrastructure, these solutions enable individuals to participate in the global economy and access opportunities for growth. Platforms like M-Pesa in Kenya and BitPesa in Africa have demonstrated the potential of mobile-based financial services to drive economic development and empower individuals.

Decentralized finance (DeFi) platforms are also playing a crucial role in promoting financial inclusion. By removing intermediaries and enabling peer-to-peer transactions, DeFi platforms create a more open and transparent financial ecosystem. Users can access a wide range of financial services, including lending, borrowing, and earning interest on digital assets, without the need for traditional banks. Projects like Compound, Aave, and MakerDAO are at the forefront of the DeFi movement, providing innovative solutions that democratize access to financial services.

Blockchain technology is also being used to address challenges related to identity verification and creditworthiness. Traditional identity verification methods are often cumbersome and exclusionary, particularly for individuals without formal identification documents. Blockchain-based digital identity solutions, like those developed by Sovrin and uPort, provide a secure and decentralized alternative, enabling individuals to manage and share their identity information with confidence. Additionally, blockchain-based credit scoring systems can provide a more accurate and inclusive assessment of an individual's creditworthiness, opening up new opportunities for access to credit.

As cryptocurrencies and blockchain technology continue to evolve, they hold the potential to create a more inclusive and equitable global financial system. By providing affordable, accessible, and transparent financial services, digital currencies can empower individuals and communities, drive economic development, and promote financial stability. The future of financial inclusion is bright, and the possibilities are limitless.

15

Chapter 15: The Cultural Impact of Cryptocurrencies

Cryptocurrencies have not only transformed the financial landscape but have also left a lasting impact on popular culture. The rise of digital currencies and blockchain technology has influenced various aspects of society, from art and entertainment to fashion and gaming. This chapter explores how crypto innovation is shaping contemporary culture and redefining societal norms.

The art world has been one of the most significant beneficiaries of the crypto revolution. The introduction of non-fungible tokens (NFTs) has transformed the way artists create, distribute, and monetize their work. Digital artists can now tokenize their creations, offering unique and verifiable pieces of art that can be bought, sold, and traded on blockchain-based marketplaces. This has democratized the art industry, allowing artists to reach a global audience and bypass traditional gatekeepers. High-profile NFT sales, such as Beeple's "Everydays: The First 5000 Days," have brought mainstream attention to the potential of digital art and established NFTs as a legitimate form of artistic expression.

The entertainment industry has also embraced the potential of blockchain technology and cryptocurrencies. Musicians, filmmakers, and content creators are leveraging NFTs to tokenize their work, offering exclusive content, experiences, and collectibles to their audiences. This new model of content distribution fosters a direct connection between creators and consumers, enabling fans to support their favorite artists and access unique offerings. Blockchain-based platforms like Audius and Mintable are leading the way in creating decentralized ecosystems for content creation and distribution.

Fashion and luxury brands are also exploring the potential of cryptocurrencies and NFTs. By tokenizing limited edition products and rare items, brands can offer exclusive digital collectibles that appeal to tech-savvy consumers. This has given rise to the concept of "digital fashion," where virtual clothing and accessories can be bought, sold, and worn in virtual environments. Brands like Gucci and Louis Vuitton have experimented with digital fashion, creating virtual items that can be used in gaming and social media platforms. The intersection of fashion and crypto is pushing the boundaries of creativity and redefining the concept of ownership and value.

The gaming industry has been one of the earliest adopters of blockchain technology and cryptocurrencies. In-game assets, such as characters, items, and land, can be tokenized as NFTs, allowing players to buy, sell, and trade these assets on blockchain-based marketplaces. This has created new economic ecosystems within virtual worlds, where players can earn real-world income through their participation. Games like Axie Infinity and Decentraland have demonstrated the potential of blockchain to create vibrant and self-sustaining digital economies, blurring the lines between virtual and real-world value.

The cultural impact of cryptocurrencies is profound, influencing various aspects of contemporary society and redefining norms. As digital currencies and blockchain technology continue to evolve, they are likely to play an increasingly important role in shaping the future of art, entertainment, fashion, and gaming. The possibilities for creative expression and innovation are boundless, and the cultural landscape will continue to be transformed by the crypto revolution.

16

Chapter 16: Lessons Learned from the Crypto Pioneers

The journey of cryptocurrencies and blockchain technology has been marked by both triumphs and setbacks. The experiences of early adopters, entrepreneurs, and investors offer valuable lessons for navigating the challenges and opportunities of the crypto space. This chapter reflects on the lessons learned from the pioneers who have shaped the industry, providing insights into the strategies and mindsets that have driven innovation and growth.

One of the key lessons from the crypto pioneers is the importance of resilience and adaptability. The early years of the cryptocurrency revolution were characterized by extreme volatility, regulatory uncertainty, and technological challenges. Despite these obstacles, pioneers like Satoshi Nakamoto, Vitalik Buterin, and Charlie Lee remained committed to their vision and continued to push the boundaries of what was possible. Their resilience and ability to adapt to changing circumstances have been instrumental in the success of their projects and the growth of the industry.

Another important lesson is the value of community and collaboration. The decentralized and open-source nature of blockchain technology has fostered a culture of collaboration and knowledge-sharing. Early adopters and developers have worked together to build and improve upon existing technologies, creating a vibrant and innovative ecosystem. The success of projects like Bitcoin, Ethereum, and Litecoin can be attributed to the collective efforts of countless individuals who have contributed to their development and growth.

Transparency and trust are also essential lessons from the crypto pioneers. The decentralized and transparent nature of blockchain technology has built trust among users, developers, and investors. By providing a verifiable and tamper-proof record of transactions, blockchain ensures the integrity of the system and reduces the risk of fraud. Projects like Bitcoin and Ethereum have gained widespread acceptance because of their commitment to transparency and security.

Innovation and experimentation are fundamental to the success of the crypto space. The pioneers of the industry have embraced a mindset of continuous improvement and experimentation, pushing the boundaries of what is possible. From the creation of new consensus algorithms to the development of decentralized applications (dApps), the crypto community has been relentless in its pursuit of innovation. This spirit of experimentation has led to groundbreaking advancements and paved the way for the future of blockchain technology.

Lastly, education and advocacy are crucial for the continued growth and acceptance of cryptocurrencies. Early adopters and industry leaders have played a vital role in educating the public, policymakers, and businesses about the benefits and potential of digital currencies. By promoting awareness and understanding, they have helped to demystify the technology and encourage its adoption. Initiatives like Bitcoin conferences, online courses, and industry publications have been instrumental in spreading knowledge and fostering a supportive community.

17

Chapter 17: Envisioning the Future of Innovation and Crypto

As we look to the future, the potential for cryptocurrencies and blockchain technology to drive further innovation and reshape our world is boundless. Emerging trends and possibilities lie ahead, from the development of new digital currencies to the integration of advanced technologies such as quantum computing. This chapter explores the exciting future of innovation and crypto, inspiring readers to imagine the limitless potential of this dynamic and transformative field.

Quantum computing is one of the most promising technologies on the horizon, with the potential to revolutionize the crypto space. Quantum computers can perform complex calculations at unprecedented speeds, enabling new levels of encryption and security for blockchain networks. The integration of quantum computing with blockchain technology could lead to the development of quantum-resistant cryptographic algorithms, ensuring the long-term security and integrity of digital currencies.

Interoperability is another key trend that will shape the future of cryptocurrencies. Currently, many blockchain networks operate in isolation, limiting their potential and creating fragmentation in the ecosystem. Efforts to develop interoperable solutions, such as cross-chain protocols and decentralized bridges, will enable seamless communication and interaction between different blockchain networks. Projects like Polkadot, Cosmos, and Chainlink are leading the way in creating a more connected and cohesive crypto ecosystem.

The rise of decentralized autonomous organizations (DAOs) and decentralized governance models will also play a crucial role in the future of innovation and crypto. DAOs enable communities to self-govern and make collective decisions without the need for intermediaries. This decentralized approach to governance has the potential to create more transparent, inclusive, and efficient decision-making processes. As DAOs continue to evolve and gain adoption, they will reshape the way organizations and communities operate.

The integration of blockchain technology with the Internet of Things (IoT) is another exciting frontier. IoT devices generate vast amounts of data that can be securely and transparently recorded on blockchain networks. This integration will enable new applications and use cases, from supply chain management and smart cities to healthcare and environmental monitoring. By leveraging the power of blockchain, IoT devices can operate with greater efficiency, security, and interoperability.

The future of innovation and crypto is bright, with limitless possibilities and opportunities for growth. As we continue to explore and harness the potential of these technologies, we can envision a world where digital currencies and blockchain drive economic development, promote financial inclusion, and create a more transparent and equitable global economy. The journey has just begun, and the future holds boundless potential for those who dare to innovate and dream.

Book Description

"The Infinite Frontier: How Billionaires Are Reinventing Countries Through Innovation and Crypto" is an exhilarating exploration of how visionary billionaires are leveraging cryptocurrencies and blockchain technology to transform the global economy. This captivating book delves into the stories of key figures like Elon Musk, Jeff Bezos, and Vitalik Buterin, who are at the forefront of this revolution. Through their investments, entrepreneurial endeavors, and public advocacy, these innovators are challenging the status quo and pushing the boundaries of what is possible.

CHAPTER 17: ENVISIONING THE FUTURE OF INNOVATION AND CRYPTO

The book provides a comprehensive overview of the rise of cryptocurrencies, the development of the blockchain ecosystem, and the profound impact of these technologies on various industries. From the democratization of financial services to the creation of decentralized governance models, the potential of crypto innovation is boundless. Readers will gain insights into the environmental implications, social impact, and cultural significance of digital currencies, as well as the lessons learned from the pioneers who have shaped the industry.

With a forward-looking perspective, "The Infinite Frontier" envisions the future of innovation and crypto, exploring emerging trends like quantum computing, interoperability, and the integration of blockchain with the Internet of Things. This thought-provoking book inspires readers to imagine the limitless potential of this dynamic and transformative field, offering a glimpse into a future where digital currencies and blockchain drive economic development, promote financial inclusion, and create a more transparent and equitable global economy.

www.ingramcontent.com/pod-product-compliance
Lightning Source LLC
LaVergne TN
LVHW020459080526
838202LV00057B/6039